Making a Natural Trumpet

Herstellung einer Naturtrompete

Making a Natural Trumpet
A Description of the International Trumpet-making Workshop

Herstellung einer Naturtrompete
Eine Beschreibung des Internationalen Trompetenbau-Workshops

Michael Münkwitz
Richard Seraphinoff
Robert Barclay

Loose Cannon Press

LIBRARY AND ARCHIVES CANADA CATALOGUING IN PUBLICATION

Münkwitz, Michael, 1956-, author
Making a natural trumpet : a description of the international
trumpet-making workshop = Herstellung einer Naturtrompete: eine
Beschreibung des Internationalen Trompetenbau-Workshops/Michael
Münkwitz, Richard Seraphinoff, Robert Barclay.

Includes bibliographical references
Text in English and German

ISBN 978-0-9936881-1-9 (pbk.)

1. Trumpet--Construction. I. Barclay, R. L. (Robert L.), author
II. Seraphinoff, Richard, author III. Title. IV. Title: Herstellung einer
Naturtrompete.

ML961.M966 2014   788.9'21923   C2014-901321-3

Published by
LOOSE CANNON PRESS

loosecannonpress@gmail.com
www.loosecannonpress.com

Table of Contents
Inhalt

Biographies
Biographien

Michael Münkwitz was trained as a brass instrument builder in Leipzig and has operated his own workshop in Rostock since 1979. His work focuses on copies of different models of trumpet from the 17th and 18th centuries. Well-known early music trumpeters play instruments from his workshop.

Michael Münkwitz erhielt seine Ausbildung zum Blechblasinstrumenten-baumeister in Leipzig und betreibt seit 1979 in Rostock seine eigene Werkstatt. Schwerpunkt seiner Arbeit sind Kopien verschiedener Trompetenmodelle des 17.-19. Jhd. Namhafte Trompeter der Alten Musik spielen Instrumente aus seiner Herstellung.

Richard Seraphinoff is Professor of Horn at the Indiana University Jacobs School of Music, where he teaches modern horn, natural horn, and courses in brass literature and history. He is also a well-known maker of historical reproductions of Baroque and Classical natural horns which are played in period instrument ensembles around the world.

Richard Seraphinoff ist Professor für Horn an der Indiana University Jacobs School of Music. Dort unterrichtet er modernes Horn, Naturhorn und Literatur und Geschichte für Blechblasinstrumente. Daneben ist er auch Hersteller von Barock- und Klassischen Naturhörnern die weltweit in Orchestern der Alten Musik gespielt werden.

Robert Barclay was born in London, England in 1946. He has a Certificate in Science Laboratory Technology, City Guilds of London Institute, 1968; a BA in Fine Arts, University of Toronto, 1975; and a PhD, Open University UK, 1999. He is a museum object restorer and trumpet-maker. Major publications: *The Care of Historic Musical Instruments, The Preservation and Use of Historic Musical Instruments,* and *The Art of the Trumpet-maker.*

Robert Barclay geboren in London, England 1946. Er hat ein Diplom in Science Laboratory Technology, City Guilds of London Institute, 1968; ein BA Fine Arts, University of Toronto, 1975; und einen PhD, Open University in Groß-britannien, 1999. Er ist Restaurator für museale Objekte und Trompetenmacher. Veröffentlichungen: *The Care of Historic Musical Instruments, The Preservation and Use of Historic Musical Instruments,* und *The Art of the Trumpet-maker.*

Section 1
Abschnitt 1

Introduction

The International Trumpet-making Workshop, which had the humble beginnings described in Section 3, has grown into an annual opportunity for trumpet players, other musicians and people with general interest from around the world, to experience the process of making a brass instrument with their own hands, using the tools and methods of the 17th century makers of Nürnberg.

The instruments produced are without compromises in construction methods. Everything we do in the workshop, with the exception of electric lights and the use of propane gas for soldering, would be more or less familiar to the guild of instrument makers of the time, although they would be envious of the quality of some of our tools and the consistency of our materials.

We have enjoyed refining the process of teaching the course, and developing ways of making the processes more accessible to the participants, and over the years the quality of the instruments produced has risen steadily. We hope the workshop will continue to be an opportunity to introduce more people to the world of making things with one's hands, and to the world of the natural trumpet as it was at the time.

Einleitung

Der Internationale Trompetenbau Workshop bietet besonders Trompetern, aber auch anderen Musikern und Interessierten aus der ganzen Welt die Möglichkeit, die Geschichte des Instrumentenbaus, die Herstellung eines Blechblasinstrumentes sowie Werkzeuge und Methoden des Nürnberger Instrumentenbaus des 17. Jahrhunderts hautnah zu erleben.

Wie in der damaligen Zeit bauen wir die Trompeten ohne Kompromisse. Die Instrumentenbauer des 17. Jahrhunderts würden unsere Methoden und Werkzeuge mit Ausnahme von elektrischem Licht und dem Einsatz von Propangas zum Löten wiedererkennen. Sicherlich wären sie ein wenig neidisch auf die Qualität unserer Werkzeuge und Materialien.

Mit Leidenschaft und Enthusiasmus haben wir in all den Jahren den Verlauf des Workshops, die Qualität der Werkzeuge und Hilfsmittel stetig verbessert. Wir hoffen, dass der Workshop auch weiterhin viele Menschen auf der Welt begeistert, die gern mit eigenen Händen ein Instrument aus der damaligen Zeit selbst anfertigen wollen.

Purpose of this Book

This book is intended as a documentation of what takes place at the International Trumpet-making Workshop, with some history of the workshop itself, historical background on the instruments and methods of

Grund dieses Buches

Dieses Buch ist eine Dokumentation über den Internationalen Trompetenbau Workshop. Es beinhaltet die Geschichte des Workshops selbst, den historischen Hintergrund zu den Instrumenten und Methoden von Hanns Hainlein und den

Hanns Hainlein and the Nürnberg brass makers of the 17th century, and other related information. The intention is to give prospective participants an idea of what is involved in the workshop and, for those who attend, to have a book documenting what they did during the week so they can remember after the fact the working methods involved.

This book, and the workshop itself, are not meant to be a set of instructions in making a trumpet, or a training session for instrument-makers. Our intention is to demonstrate how the original instrument-makers worked with the materials and tools of their time, but also to keep these techniques alive.

There is nothing taking place in the workshop that is not documented in this book, because the teachers would like to emphasize that we feel there are no 'trade secrets' in the making of historical brass instruments, other than starting with a good design and doing high quality work with good materials and tools without modern compromises. Dimensions are intentionally not given in this book, since details are available from the collections that hold the originals. However, participants in the workshop are free to take whatever information on the dimensions and construction techniques of our rendition of the Hainlein trumpet that they wish.

Nürnberger Instrumentenbauern des 17. Jahrhunderts und weitere Informationen. Die Absicht ist, Interessierten die Arbeitsschritte vorzustellen und zu zeigen, was sie im Workshop erwartet. Für aktive Teilnehmer bietet es eine Dokumentation zur Erinnerung an die Herstellung einer eigenen Naturtrompete.

Dieses Buch ist nicht als Anleitung zum Bau einer Trompete oder als Lehrbuch für Auszubildende gedacht obwohl die beschriebenen Methoden und Werkzeuge für Instrumentenbauer sicher interessant sind. Auch soll der Workshop nicht als Ausbildung zum Instrumentenbauer verstanden werden.

Wir wollen mit den traditionellen und historischen Handwerkstechniken zeigen, wie die alten Meister mit ihren damaligen Möglichkeiten hervorragende Musikinstrumente gebaut haben und diese Tradition für die Nachwelt bewahren. Alles, was im Workshop passiert, ist hier in diesem Buch dokumentiert. Wir haben ausdrücklich keine „Geschäftsgeheimnisse", außer einer guten Vorlage, Arbeiten von hoher Qualität mit gutem Material und Werkzeugen, ohne moderne Kompromisse. Maße sind hier bewusst nicht angegeben, da wir meinen, jeder Interessierte kann in den öffentlichen Sammlungen Instrumente vermessen und Dokumentationen studieren. Alle Informationen zum Nachbau der „Hainlein"-Trompete sind den Teilnehmern im Workshop zugänglich.

The Hanns Hainlein Trumpet of 1632

Nürnberg, in southern Germany, was a centre of metal manufacture since at least the Middle Ages, and it had been suggested that some sort of industrial work had taken place there in an

Die Trompete von Hanns Hainlein, 1632

Nürnberg im Süden Deutschlands war ein Zentrum der Verarbeitung von Metallen seit dem Mittelalter und vermutlich in einer ungebrochenen Linie seit vorchristlicher Zeit. Die Stadt

unbroken line since Classical times. The city was conveniently situated on a north-south trade route between Italy and the northern countries and was in fairly close proximity to supplies of raw materials, while the River Pegnitz provided an endless source of waterpower for the machines of the many industries situated there.

As a result of the continuous commerce at this cross-road, Nürnberg became an intellectual centre with developments in mathematics, science and cartography, attracting artists and philosophers from across the German speaking countries and beyond. It also became the favoured residence for the Imperial Court during the heyday of the Holy Roman Empire. Products of the many workshops included mathematical and surveying instruments, weapons and armour, brass utensils of all kinds, decorative religious objects, and a wide range of musical instruments.

In Hanns Hainlein's time—the early part of the 17th century—an influential guild of brass instrument-makers was well established, and their output accounted for the lion's share of trumpets purchased throughout Europe. Instruments for art music made only a small portion of the production, the larger number being trumpets destined for use at court or in battle. The almost perpetual state of warfare in Europe at this period ensured the demand for a large and steady volume of martial instruments.

Hanns Hainlein, the son of Sebastian (1559-1631) also a brass instrument-maker, was born in 1596 and died in 1671, which is a considerable lifespan for a craftsman of that period. There are several instruments extant with his name upon them, but the 1632 trumpet appears to be the earliest. One of his apprentices, who went on to open a workshop of his own, was Wolfram Birckholtz, one of whose trumpets was found hanging in the church in Belitz

befand sich wirtschaftlich günstig an der Nord-Süd-Handelsroute zwischen Italien und den nördlichen Ländern und war damit auch in unmittelbarer Nähe zur Rohstoffversorgung. Der Fluss Pegnitz bot eine Quelle der Wasserkraft für Maschinen der verschiedenen Branchen der Metallverarbeitung.

Als Ergebnis des kontinuierlichen Handels an diesem Standort wurde Nürnberg auch ein geistiges Zentrum der Mathematik, Naturwissenschaften und Kartographie. Nürnberg zog Künstler und Philosophen aus dem gesamten deutschsprachigen Raum und darüber hinaus an. Die Stadt wurde das bevorzugte Quartier für den kaiserlichen Hof in der Blütezeit des Heiligen Römischen Reiches. Produkte der vielen Meisterwerkstätten sind mathematische und Vermessungsinstrumente, Waffen und Rüstungen, Messinggegenstände aller Art, dekorative religiöse Gegenstände sowie eine Vielzahl von Musikinstrumenten.

In der Zeit Hanns Hainleins, Anfang des 17.Jahrhunderts, war die Zunft der Blechblasinstrumentenbauer etabliert und sehr einflussreich. Diese Zunft lieferte den Löwenanteil ihrer Trompeten nach ganz Europa. Die Instrumente für die Kunstmusik machten nur einen kleinen Teil der Produktion aus; der weitaus größere Anteil war für den Einsatz am Hof und für die Schlacht bestimmt. Die fast ständigen militärischen Auseinandersetzungen und Kriege in Europa zu dieser Zeit sicherten eine große Nachfrage an Instrumenten für das Militär.

Hanns Hainlein, Sohn von Sebastian Hainlein (1559-1631), der ebenfalls Blechblasinstrumentenbauer war, wurde 1596 geboren und starb im Jahre 1671, was eine beträchtlich lange Lebensdauer für einen Handwerker der damaligen Zeit war. Es sind noch verschiedene Instrumente aus seiner Werkstatt erhalten, doch die Trompete

(see below). The family name Hainlein continued through Paul, Hanns's nephew, and Paul's son Michael.

The Hainlein trumpet of 1632 falls in the period of Girolamo Fantini's *Modo per imparare a sonare di tromba* (1638), a seminal publication that opened the way to playing art music on the instrument. Like many of the instruments that have survived from this period, the trumpet is well-made and shows signs of being taken care of, although it is impossible now to know who played it and for what genre of music it was intended and used.

There were two reasons for choosing and staying with the Hanns Hainlein design of 1632 for the duration of the ITW. First and foremost is the simplicity of the design itself. The bell flare is easier to form due to its gentler, more Renaissance shape than the later more flared bell designs of the 18th century, which involve much more stretching of the metal at the anvil. Beginners can successfully complete the Hainlein bell in a few labour-intensive hours of work.

The second reason for the Hainlein design has to do with our friendly working relationship with professional instrument makers, who are producing copies of trumpets of the 18th century that are used by players around the world in period instrument ensembles. Initially, several makers were taken aback that we would give participants the information to make instruments, and then send them home with playable examples. The initial assumption was that this would make it unnecessary for our participants to become customers of the makers of fine copies. As the workshop progressed it became obvious that the opposite was true, and that the natural trumpet of the 17th century made by participants in the workshop was a great introduction to the instrument. This process actually encourages a greater knowledge of the natural trumpet, which in turn is good for the

von 1632 scheint die früheste zu sein. Einer seiner Lehrlinge, der später eine eigene Werkstatt in Nürnberg eröffnete, war Wolff Birckholtz. Seine vermutlich erste Trompete wurde in der Kirche zu Belitz gefunden (s.u.). Der Familienname „Hainlein" wurde durch seinen Neffen Paul und dessen Sohn Michael fortgesetzt.

Die Hainlein-Trompete 1632 fällt in die Zeit von Girolamo Fantini's „Modo per imparare a sonare di tromba (1638)", einer Publikation zum Beginn des Weges zur Kunstmusik auf diesem Instrument. Wie viele erhaltene Instrumente aus dieser Zeit ist diese Trompete meisterlich gebaut und wurde sorgfältig behandelt. Dennoch konnten selbst Historiker nicht herausfinden wer das Instrument geblasen hat und für welche Art von Musik es bestimmt war.

Es gab zwei Gründe, sich für die Trompete von Hanns Hainlein 1632 als Vorlage für den ITW zu entscheiden. Erstens und hauptsächlich gab das einfache Modell selbst den Ausschlag. Der Schallbecher („Renaissance-Form") lässt sich leichter formen als die späteren Schallbecher des 18. Jahrhunderts, bei denen die Dehnungen des Materials am Amboss weit schwieriger gestaltet. Die Teilnehmer können das Hainlein-Schallstück bereits nach ein paar intensiven Arbeitsstunden in die entsprechende Form bringen.

Der zweite Grund für das Hainlein-Modell ist unsere freundschaftliche Verbindung zu vielen professionellen Trompetenbauern, die Kopien von Instrumenten des 18.Jahrhunderts für Spieler und Ensembles in der ganzen Welt herstellen. Zunächst waren viele Kollegen erstaunt, dass wir den Teilnehmern alle Informationen zu dem Instrument geben und sie mit einer spielbaren Trompete nach Hause fahren lassen. Ursprünglich überwog die Angst, potentielle Kunden zu verlieren. Doch die Entwicklung des ITW machte

entire community of instrument-makers and players. Also, because the Hainlein bell form is markedly different from the typical 18th century profile, there was no competition with the makers producing instruments that are used regularly in period instrument ensembles for the high baroque music of Bach, Handel, and many others.

deutlich: Das Gegenteil ist der Fall. Die Trompeten der Teilnehmer des Workshops bieten einen tollen Einstieg in die Kenntnisse und Zusammenhänge des Naturtrompetenspiels und das wiederum ist gut für die gesamte Gemeinschaft der Spieler und Instrumentenbauer. Die Schallstück-form der Hainlein-Trompete unter-scheidet sich deutlich von den typischen Formen des 18.Jahrhunderts, den meist kopierten Instrumenten der Kollegen, für die hohe Barockmusik von Bach, Händel und vielen anderen Komponisten für Solisten und Ensembles.

Abschnitt 2
Section 2

Die Prozesse in Bildern
The Processes in Pictures

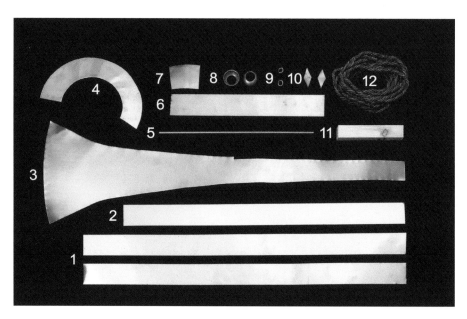

Abb 1. Closeup alle Teile
Fig 1. Close-up of all the parts

Alle Teile zu Beginn des Workshops	The parts at the start of the workshop

1	Zuschnitt Rohre	1	Strips for tubes
2	Zuschnitt Rohr für Bögen	2	Strips for bows
3	Zuschnitt Schallstück	3	Bell piece
4	Zuschnitt Kranz	4	Garland piece
5	Halbrunddraht für Kranz	5	Half-round wire for garland
6	Zuschnitt Hülsen	6	Strip for ferrules
7	Zuschnitt Knaufhülse	7	Piece for ball ferrule
8	Teile für Knauf	8	Ball halves
9	Ösen	9	Rings
10	Platten	10	Saddles for rings
11	Holzblock	11	Wood block
12	Kordel	12	Cord

Abb 2. Eine „Phase" am Zuschnitt des Schallstücks an beiden Seiten der späteren Verzahnung feilen. Ca.4mm breit
Fig 2. Filing the edge of the bell where the toothed seam will engage. It is filed to a knife edge about 4mm wide before cutting the teeth

Abb 3. Mit dem Zirkel eine Abstandslinie ca. 4mm vom Rand markieren und „Zähne" bis zu dieser Markierung einschneiden. Die Lotnaht ist später sichtbar, daher sind gleichmäßige „Zähne" wichtig
Fig 3. The depth of the teeth is marked with dividers, then the teeth are cut with tinsnips. The solder join is visible later, so the teeth should be cut accurately

Abb 4. Die „Zähne" abwechselnd in V-Form mit einer Zange auseinander biegen
Fig 4. The teeth are bent inwards and outwards in a V-shape with pliers

Abb 5. Den Zuschnitt über eine Stange an der gedachten Mittellinie biegen.
Achtung, scharfe Kanten und Zähne, Verletzungsgefahr!
Fig 5. The bell piece is bent over a steel mandrel. The teeth and the edges of the bell
piece are very sharp!

Abb 6. Ein „Zahn" unten, ein „Zahn" oben wird das Blech wie ein Reißverschluss zusammengefügt. Die Flachfeile ist ein gutes Hilfsmittel
Fig 6. The teeth are engaged with each other, alternating over and under. The end of a file is useful for pushing the teeth together

Abb 7. Mit dem Holzhammer die Lotnaht auf der Stange glätten und endgültig fest zusammenfügen
Fig 7. The teeth are tapped tightly together using a wooden mallet, with the bell laid on a steel mandrel

Abb 8. Flussmittel „Borax" zum Hartlöten auf die Naht auftragen. Mit Silberlot die Lotnaht löten. Wichtig ist ein gleichmäßiger Fluß des Silberlotes, damit keine Löcher in der Naht bleiben, bzw. die „Zähne" sich später nicht öffnen
Fig 8. The seam is coated with borax flux and silver soldered. The solder is very fluid, so to ensure that it flows completely and that there are no gaps that might appear later, it is important to make the seam very tight

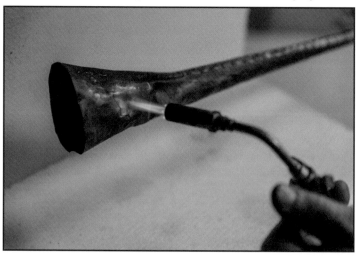

Abb 9. Durch Hämmern und drücken wird das Material hart. In Abständen muss daher das Schallstück geglüht, also wieder weich gemacht werden. Eine gute Rotfärbung ist das Zeichen für die richtige Glühtemperatur
Fig 9. During hammering and burnishing brass hardens, so the bell must be heated and then quenched in water to soften it. A low red colour is sufficient

*Abb 10. Nur bis ca. 5 cm vom Rand den Schallbecher auf dem Amboss hämmern.
Das Material wird dadurch geweitet und nach etlichen Wiederholungen erhält das
Schallstück seine gewünschte Form und Größe*
*Fig 10. Only the first 5cm or so of the bell is hammered. The material is stretched
and, after about five iterations, it gets its desired shape and size*

*Abb 11. Nur mit dem Gummihammer das Schallstück auf dem Schallstückeisen
„rund" und in Form hämmern*
*Fig 11. The bell is laid on the bell mandrel and hammered round with a rubber
mallet. A steel hammer is never used directly on the bell mandrel*

Abb 12. Mittels einer Stange das Schallstück andrücken, weiten und Stück für
Stück auf die gewünschte Größe bringen. Wichtig ist, dass das Material auf der
Stange aufliegt und nicht „hohl" gerieben wird. Liegt das Material auf der Stange,
wird es durch den Druck geweitet, liegt es nicht auf („hohl") wird es reduziert
Fig 12. The bell is burnished on the mandrel with a steel rod. It is important that
the brass is in good contact with the mandrel, with no hollow space below. Good
contact ensures expansion of the brass; poor contact will cause reduction in size

Abb 13. Die gleichmäßig geschlossene Lotnaht auf einer konischen Stange mit
einem Metallhammer verhämmern. Die „doppelte" Wandstärke der Verzahnung
wird dadurch reduziert und einheitliche Materialstärke erreicht. Ein Bleiklotz
dient als Unterlage
Fig 13. The seam is hammered with a steel hammer on a conical mandrel laid on a
lead block. In this way the extra thickness around the teeth is reduced

*Abb 14. Ist der richtige Schallbecher Durchmesser erreicht und das Blech liegt
überall gut und gleichmäßig auf der Schallstückstange an, die Lotnaht feilen. Zum
Abschluss die gesamte Oberfläche mit einem Dreikantschaber schaben
Fig 14. Once the bell is the right size, and the metal lies evenly on the mandre, the
solder seam is filed down and the surface finished by scraping*

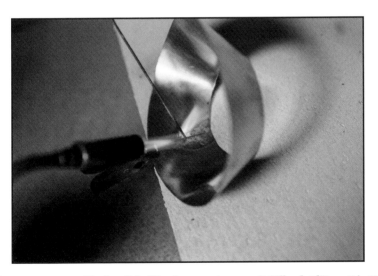

*Abb 15. Den Kranz für den Schallbecher von innen mit Silberlot löten. Die Naht
wird stumpf zusammen gelötet
Fig 15. The bell garland is silver-soldered together. This is a butt seam, soldered
from the inside*

Abb 16. Den Halbrunddraht auch mit Silberlot löten und dann mit dem Holzhammer am Konus der Schallstückstange anpassen
Fig 16. The half-round wire for the bezel is bent round, and the ends silver-soldered together. The ring is tapped with a wooden mallet on the bell mandrel to make it completely round

Abb 17. Mit einer Stahlnadel Markierungen setzen: 1) für die Position des Halbrunddrahtes und 2) als Markierung für die Zacken
Fig 17. Using a steel point to mark: 1) the position of the bezel and 2) the placing of the decorations

Abb 18. Mit einer Spezialhalterung („Spinne") den Halbrunddraht fixieren und mit Zinnlot weich löten
Fig 18. Using a special jig to hold it firmly onto the garland, the bezel is soft soldered in place

Abb 19. Mit dem Dreikantschaber die Zinnlotreste beseitigen
Fig 19. The excess solder is removed from the seam with a triangular scraper

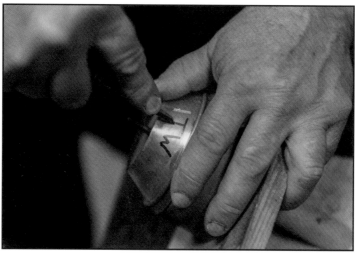

Abb 20. Mit diversen Graviersticheln verewigt sich der Instrumentenbauer ganz individuell, zum Beispiel mit Namen, Datum, Ort und verschiedenen Mustern und Verzierungen
Fig 21. Using a variety of engravers, makers may engrave their names, dates, location and other details

Abb 21. Auch die Verzierungen mit Zacken gehören zur Dekoration. Es empfiehlt sich vorher eine genaue Markierung
Fig 21. The points cut on the garland are decorative. They are marked accurately with a pair of dividers

Abb 22. Der überstehende Rand am Halbrunddraht wird mit einer speziellen Zange gebogen...
Fig 22. The projecting edge of the garland is folded over with smooth-jawed pliers...

Abb 23. ...das Schallstück in den Kranz gesteckt und fixiert, damit Lotnaht-Kranz auf der gleichen Stelle wie Lotnaht-Schallstück ist. Stück für Stück wird mit einem kleinen Kugelhammer der Rand des Kranzes weiter umgebördelt. Das Schallstück ist fertig !
Fig 23. ...then the garland is placed on the bell with its solder seam over the seam on the bell, and the edge is incrementally hammered over until tight. The bell is now finished!

Abb 24. Die Messingstreifen für die Rohre und Bögen um eine Stange biegen
Fig 24. The brass strips for the tubes and bows are bent over a steel mandrel

Abb 25. Mit den Daumen die Kanten stumpf, also nicht überlappend,
zusammendrücken
Fig 25. The strips of brass for the tubes are bent around on a mandrel so the edges
butt against each other, and are not overlapped

18

Abb 26. Mit dem Holzhammer die Naht glätten...
Fig 26. With a wooden mallet the seam is tapped down...

Abb 27. ...und mit einer Stange glatt reiben. Die beiden Kanten müssen
gleichmäßig geschlossen sein
Fig 27. ...and with a burnisher the edges are brought together. The seam must be
totally closed with no gap showing

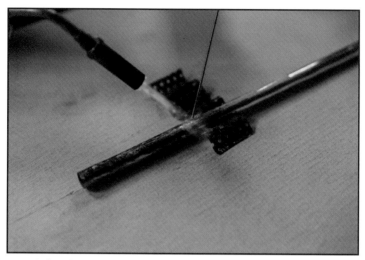

Abb 28. Wie bei dem Schallstück wird auch bei den Rohren als Flußmittel zum Hartlöten Borax aufgetragen. Mit Silberlot die Naht löten
Fig 28. In the same way as the bell, the seam is coated with borax flux and silver-soldered

Abb 29. Nach dem Löten die Lotnaht auf einer Stange glatt reiben und mit einer Feile von Lotresten befreien. Damit das Rohr ohne Komplikationen durch das Zieheisen gezogen werden kann, ist eine sehr sorgfältige Kontrolle der Oberfläche wichtig (keine Lotreste)
Fig 29. After soldering the seam, the tube is returned to the mandrel and burnished down. Lumps of solder are filed off. The tube must be really smooth so it will pass through the die in the following process

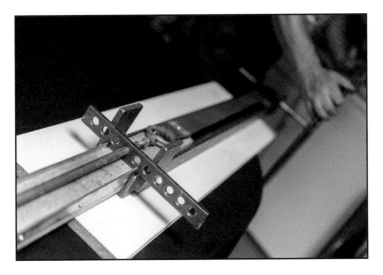

Abb 30. Das Rohr auf eine Stange stecken und diese mit dem Gurt der Ziehbank befestigen. Per Hand nun das Rohr durch das Locheisen ziehen. Das Resultat: Das Rohr ist rund, hat den gewünschten Rohrdurchmesser und eine glatte Oberfläche
Fig 30. The tube, on a mandrel, is pulled by hand through a drawplate. This results in a smooth tube of exactly the right diameter

Abb 31. Mit dem Dreikantschaber die Oberfläche der beiden langen Rohre schaben. Das Rohr für die Bögen wird erst nach dem Biegen geschabt
Fig 31. The two long tubes are finished with a triangular scraper. The tubes for the bows are left until after they are bent

Abb 32. Durch den Ziehvorgang ist das Rohr wieder hart.
Das Rohr für die Bögen halbieren und im Bereich des Biegens glühen. Zu beachten
ist, die Lotnaht zeigt nach hinten! Eine direkte Flamme öffnet die Naht, das
Silberlot schmilzt
Fig 32. The bows are made from a long tube cut in half. After drawing, the brass is
very hard and must be annealed. The section to be bent is heated on the back,
keeping the heat away from the seam to avoid melting the solder

Abb 33. Ein Ende des Rohres mit einem Kork verschließen und danach mit
siedenden Wasser zur Erwärmung füllen...
Fig 33. A cork is inserted in one end of the tube, and the tube is then filled with hot
water...

Abb 34. ...und danach mit flüssigen Cerrobend. Im kalten Wasser sofort abkühlen
Fig 34. ...and then the tube is filled with Cerrobend and quickly cooled in water

Abb 35. Im Biegemodell das Rohr mit einer Zange fixieren und mit einem Rohrstück verlängern. Die Lotnaht zeigt nach oben. Gefühlvoll das Rohr in kleinen Schritten biegen...
Fig 35. The tube is held in place with a Visegrip, with the seam upwards. An extra length of pipe is used to give better leverage. Then gentle bending begins...

Abb 36. ...nächster Schritt das Rohre ist Halb gebogen...
Fig 36. ...next step, the tube is half bent...

Abb 37. ...nächster Schritt fast fertig...
Fig 37. ...next step, nearly done...

Abb 38. ...und fertig.
Fig 38. ...and finished.

Abb 39. Die Falten auf der Innenseite des Bogens mit einem Kugelhammer verhämmern. Als Unterlage dient wieder der Bleiklotz. Das Cerrobend ist noch nicht ausgeschmolzen!
Fig 39. Small wrinkles on the inside curve are tapped out with a hammer using a block of lead to support the bow. The tube is still filled with Cerrobend!

Abb 40. Die Außenseite des Bogens glätten...
Fig 40. The outer side of the bow is burnished...

Abb 41. ...auch die Innenseite. Durch das Glätten wird die Oberfläche nicht nur
gleichmäßig sondern auch wieder hart. Nach diesem Arbeitsschritt das Cerobent
in heißem Wasser ausschmelzen
Fig 41. ...then the inside surface. The burnishing smooths the metal but also work-
hardens it. Finally, the Cerrobend is melted out under hot water

Abb 42. Den Ring aus Messingdraht mit Silberlot auf die Platte löten...
Fig 42. A ring of brass wire is silver-soldered onto its saddle...

Abb 43. ...und mit Zinnlot auf die Bögen löten
Fig 43. ...and attached to the bow with soft solder

*Abb 44. Mit dem Dreikantschaber wieder die Zinnlotreste beseitigen und mit
Schleifband die Lötstelle schleifen*
*Fig 44. The excess solder is removed with a triangular scraper, then the bow is
finished with abrasive paper*

*Abb 45. Stumpf zusammenfügen des Blechs für die Hülse vom Knauf wie bei den
Rohren*
*Fig 45. The part for the ball sleeve is wrapped around a tapered mandrel and the
edges brought together in the same way as the tubes*

Abb 46. Mit Silberlot die Naht schließen
Fig 46. The seam is silver-soldered

Abb 47. Die Lotnaht feilen und glätten
Fig 47. The seam is filed and burnished

Abb 48. Mit einem Gravierstichel Ringe als Verzierung einstechen, sowie Markierungen für die Zähne auf beiden Seiten auftragen
Fig 48. The decorative rings are marked with an engraver, while the placement of the teeth is marked with a black pen at each end

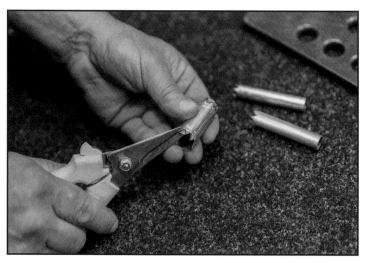

Abb 49. Zähne einschneiden und Verzierungen mit Punzen und kleiner Rundfeile anbringen. (s. Abb 55)
Fig 49. The teeth for all ferrules are cut with tinsnips. The teeth will be decorated further (see Fig 55)

Abb 50. Beide Halbrundteile für den Knauf mit Silberlot löten und...
Fig 50. The two halves of the ball are silver-soldered together and...

Abb 51. ...die Naht mit einer Feile von Lotresten befreien und eine gleichmäßige
Oberfläche feilen
Fig 51. ...the excess solder is filed off and the whole surface brought to a uniform
appearance

Abb 52. Bohrung mit Dreikantschaber oder Halbrundfeile erweitern bis die Kugel mittig auf der Hülse sitzt. Kugel mit Zinnlot auf die Hülse löten
Fig 52. The hole is enlarged with a triangular scraper or half-round file until it fits the sleeve perfectly. The ball will be attached to the sleeve with soft solder

Abb 53. Sägen der Hülsen auf entsprechende Längen. Es gibt zwei kurze und drei lange Hülsen
Fig 53. The ferrules are sawn to the correct length. There are two short ferrules and three long ones

Abb 54. „Einstiche" mit dem Gravierstichel, wie bei der Knaufhülse, sind dekorative Verzierungen. Nur auf eine Seite der Hülse kommt die Markierung für die Zähne
Fig 54. Rings are engraved on the ferrule and the placement of the teeth is marked with a black pen at one end only

Abb 55. „Spiegel" an die Zähne mit kleiner Rundfeile anbringen. Diese optionale Dekoration findet sich auch am Schallstückkranz und der Knaufhülse wieder.
Fig 55. A small round file is used to decorate the teeth. These decorations will also appear on the ball sleeve and the bell garland

Abb 56. Die auf gewünschte Länge gesägten Rohre auf einer Seite konisch pressen.
Bei der späteren Montage der Trompete werden die Rohre, Bögen und das
Schallstück zusammengesteckt. Die Teile werden nicht gelötet
Fig 56. One end of of the long tubes and the bows is tapered inwards. In the
following pictures the whole assembly can be seen

Abb 57. Eine Seite des Bogens ebenfalls konisch pressen
Fig 57. One end of each bow is tapered inwards

Abb 58. Eine lange Hülse über das andere Ende des Rohres stecken und dann vorsichtig weiten. Auch das Ende des Schallstücks mit einer langen Hülse weiten
Fig 58. A long ferrule is placed on the end of one of the long tubes, and the tube is expanded outwards to receive the tapered end of the bow

Abb 59. Eine kurze Hülse auf Bogen stecken und gefühlvoll weiten
Fig 59. A short ferrule is placed on one side of the bow, which is then expanded outwards

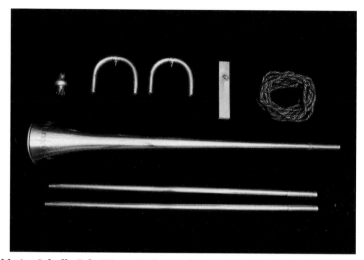

Abb 60. Schallstück, Bögen, Rohre und Knauf sind fertig für die Montage:
Schallstück—Bogen—Rohr—Bogen—Rohr.
Fixieren des Holzblocks zwischen Schall und Rohr...
Fig 60. The bell, bows, tubes and ball are ready for assembly in order: bell—bow—
lower tube—bow—upper tube (mouthpipe). The wood block is fitted between the
bell and the mouthpipe...

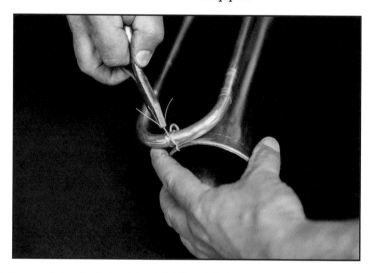

Abb 61. ...und durch ein Loch im Schallstück befestigt, mit einem Messingdraht
Bogen—Schallstück verbinden
Fig 61. ...and the bell is attached to the bow with brass wire through a hole drilled
in the bell rim

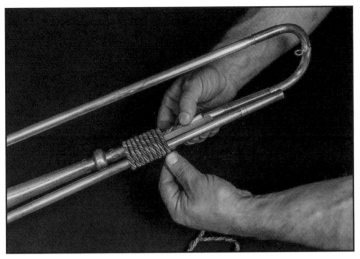

Abb 62. Die Kordel um den Holzblock fest wickeln. Damit erhält die Trompete Stabilität und ein gutes Aussehen
Fig 62. The wood block is bound with cord, which stabilizes the instrument and gives it a nice appearance

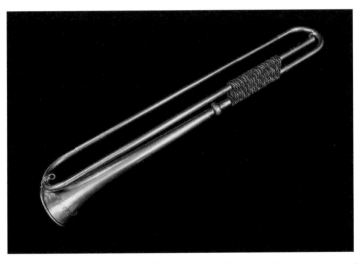

Abb 63. Was am Montag noch als Blech auf der Werkbank lag, ist nun nach einer Woche spannender und harter Arbeit endlich eine wunderschöne Naturtrompete.
Fig 63. What started as a set of brass pieces on the workbench on Monday is now, with a week of hard work, a wonderful natural trumpet

Spezialwerkzeuge
Special Tools

Abb 64. Drehmaschine zum Drehen der Zierringe am Knauf
Fig 64. Lathe for turning decorative rings on the ball

Abb 65. Drehmaschine zum Drehen der Zierringe an den Hülsen
Fig 65. Lathe for turning decorative rings on the ferrules

Abb 66. Drehmaschine zur Markierung der Position für den halbrunddracht auf dem Kranz und zum Drehen der Zierringe
Fig 66. Lathe for marking the position of the bell rim on the garland and for turning decorative rings

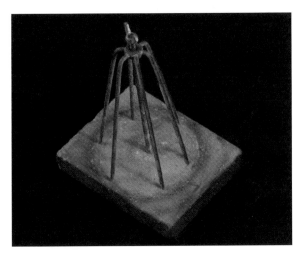

Abb 67. Spannvorrichtung zum Halten des halbrunddrachtes auf dem Kranz beim Löten
Fig 67. Jig for holding the bell rim in place when soldering

Abb 68. Kegelstange zum Öffnen der Rohrer, und konische Presse zur Reduktion der entsprechenden Enden
Fig 68. Tapered mandrel for opening the ends of tubes, and a tapered squeezer for reducing the corresponding ends

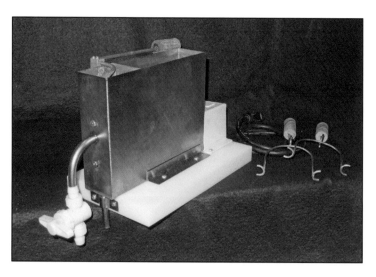

Abb 69. Thermostatisch gesteuerter Tank für Cerrobend
Fig 69. Thermostatically controlled tank for Cerrobend

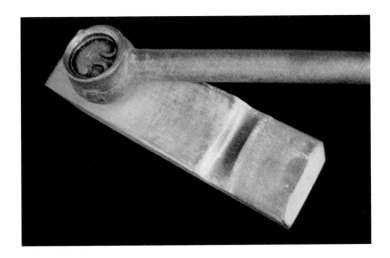

Abb 70. Poliermaschine zum Glätten der Bögen
Fig 70. Burnisher for smoothing the bows

Abb 71. Biegernvorrichtung zum Biegen der Bögen mit abnehmbaren Abschnitten
Fig 71. Jig for bending the bows, with removable sections

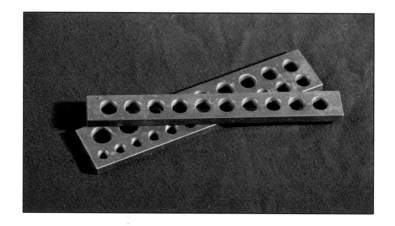

Abb 72. Locheisen für reduzierende Komponenten
Fig 72. Drawplates for reducing components

Abb 73. Verwenden Sie immer den richtigen Hammer!
Fig 73. Always use the correct hammer!

Abb 74. Zufriedene Workshop-Teilnehmer
Fig 74. Satisfied workshop participants

Bis auf wenige Ausnahmen wurde das Instrument nach historischen und
traditionellen Arbeitstechniken gefertigt, wie sie die alten Meister vor über 350
Jahren angewendet haben
Through the use of traditional and historic handwork techniques, and with very
little compromise, the trumpet-making craft of 350 years ago has been reproduced

Section 3
Abschnitt 3

History of the Workshop
Geschichte der Workshop

The idea for what was to become the International Trumpet-making Workshop arose in 1993. Bob Barclay had met Rick Seraphinoff that year at the Historic Brass Society annual conference in Amherst, Massachusetts. After Bob's presentation on historic instrument-making techniques, Rick became interested in observing the process of making a bell by hammering and burnishing. Later that year he drove up to Ottawa, Ontario and spent a couple of days watching Bob zipping up bells and whacking them out on the anvil.

It wasn't long before a letter arrived from Rick suggesting that the two of them offer a workshop in Bloomington, Indiana, the idea being to spend a week instructing eight or ten participants in making natural trumpets. Back in the mid-1970s Bob had been involved with the Early Music Workshop at Scarborough College near Toronto, teaching workshops on making Renaissance slide trumpets. He had used drawn, seamless tubing, a very simple bell design, and many other time-saving dodges. Even so, it was a week of hard labour with musically and historically dubious results. Rick's proposed workshop would offer instruments made with historical techniques wherever possible, which is an order of magnitude more complicated and time-consuming. Bob estimated at the time that in his private trumpet-making workshop he could complete an instrument in 25 hours, and now the participants–some very likely with little previous experience–would be

Die Idee für den Internationalen Trompetenbau Workshop entstand im Jahre 1993. Bob Barclay hielt bei der jährlichen Historic Brass Society Tagung in Amherst (MA) einen Vortrag über die Methoden des historischen Trompetenbaus. Nach diesem Vortrag war Rick Seraphinoff sehr begeistert und fragte Robert, ob er die Herstellung eines Schallstücks nach diesen Techniken beobachten könnte. Rick fuhr im gleichen Jahr nach Ottawa (Ontario) und besuchte Bob für ein paar Tage in seiner Werkstatt und erlebte hautnah die Entstehung eines Trompetenschallstücks nach historischen Methoden.

Es dauerte nicht lange, bis Bob einen Brief von Rick bekam, in dem er vorschlug, einen Trompetenbauworkshop in Bloomington (Indiana) anzubieten, mit der Absicht, in einer Woche mit bis zu 10 Teilnehmern eine Trompete nach diesen Techniken herzustellen. Mitte der 1970-iger Jahre hatte Robert schon beim Early Music Workshop im Scarborough College in der Nähe von Toronto zum Thema Zugtrompete der Renaissance einen Workshop geleitet. Damals verwendeten sie nahtloses Rohr, ein einfaches Schallstück, u.a. um Zeit zu sparen. Trotzdem war es eine Woche harter Arbeit und das Ergebnis war musikalisch und instrumentenbaulich nicht ganz befriedigend. Ricks Vorschlag bot nun eine Chance, mit historischen Methoden so gut wie möglich mit den alten Techniken eine bessere Qualität und ein authentischeres Ergebnis als bisher zu erreichen. Bob benötigt ca. 25

44

expected to do the same thing in less than half that time. Bob was therefore highly skeptical that this could be accomplished. Neither of them remembers the point at which it was decided this crazy scheme would go ahead, but once the decision was made it was simply a question of Bob packing every tool he could think of into a large wooden crate and driving the 1400kms from Ottawa, Ontario to Bloomington, Indiana.

The first trumpet-making workshop took place in 1994 at the silversmithing workshop at Indiana University. Bob recalls telling the eight victims on the first day of the workshop that the chances of completing an instrument were remote, but we would have a lot of fun trying. So, their emotions when they heard eight completed trumpets being sounded at noon on the sixth day of the workshop can only be imagined! When comparing the tooling used at that time with today's equipment, one can only marvel that anything remotely musical could have emerged. The credit must go to Hanns Hainlein whose instrument provided such an excellent model.

The teachers sometimes wonder over a glass of red wine in the evening what Herr Hainlein would have thought had he known.

The 1995 workshop was conducted in the silversmithing shop at IU again, and at the end of this second year it was becoming evident that this was not just a flash in the pan. Word-of-mouth publicity meant that participants were booking in advance for future work-shops. For the third year the workshop was moved to the Hoosier Hills Career Center in Bloomington, a vocational technical school that offered more spacious facilities. It was at this time that Friedemann Immer approached Rick and Bob, requesting a workshop at the Sweelincks Conservatorium in Amsterdam for the summer of 1996.

Arbeitsstunden für die Herstellung einer Trompete. Die Frage war, ob die Teilnehmer, ohne Erfahrungen im Instrumentenbau in ca. 40 Stunden ein solches Instrument bauen können. Bob war sehr skeptisch, Rick dagegen sehr optimistisch, das zu erreichen. Beide können sich nicht mehr erinnern, wann die Entscheidung fiel, dieses verrückte Projekt zu wagen. Nach der Entscheid-ung für einen Workshop musste Robert nur noch die Werkzeuge und Materialien in eine große Holzkiste verpacken und die 1.400 km von Ottawa nach Bloomington im Auto zurücklegen.

Der erste Trompetenbau Workshop fand 1994 in der Silberschmiedewerkstatt der Indiana Universität statt. Bob erinnert sich, dass er den ersten acht „Opfern" nicht versprechen konnte, nach einer Woche eine fertige Trompete in der Hand zu halten, Ihnen dafür aber viel Freude und Spaß bei der Arbeit garantierte. Der Leser kann sich kaum vorstellen, wie groß die Freude am 6. Tag war, als alle Trompeten spielbar fertiggestellt waren! Wenn wir die sehr primitiven Werkzeuge vom ersten Workshop mit den heutigen Werk-zeugen und Hilfsmitteln vergleichen, sind wir immer noch erstaunt über das gute Ergebnis. Dafür müssen wir uns bei Hanns Hainlein bedanken, dass er uns eine so gute Vorlage geliefert hat.

Am Abend, bei einem Glas Rotwein, träumen wir von der Reaktion Hainleins auf unsere Arbeit, die auf seinen Ideen beruht.

1995 fand wieder der Trompetenbau Workshop in der Silberschmiedewerk-statt an der Indiana Universität statt. Am Ende dieses zweiten Jahres war bereits klar, dass es nicht nur ein kurzzeitiger Spaß war. Durch die Mund-zu-Mund-Werbung wollten mehr Interessierte am Workshop teilnehmen. Ab dem dritten Jahr wurde der Work-shop im Hoosier Hills Career Center, einem technischen Ausbildungszentrum

They look upon those times now and wonder how they ever had the nerve to pack everything needed into a single wooden crate, to be flown from Ottawa on the same KLM flight Bob would take. It worked, but it was extremely improvised. Credit goes to Friedemann for the invitation, and for having the organizational energy and connections in the European baroque trumpet world to see it through. It is quite probable that without Friedemann the now international trumpet-making workshop would never have become established in Europe.

The year 1997 saw three turning points. There were back-to-back European workshops that year; the first was in Nürnberg organized by Edward Tarr and hosted by the Germanisches Nationalmuseum, while the second was a return to Amsterdam. The first turning point, at the close of the workshop in Nürnberg, was the first official post-workshop performance on the completed instruments. This was a public concert, staged in the galleries of the museum's musical instrument collection. Among the pieces played were an *Intrada Imperiale* by Girolamo Fantini and the *Sonata Sancti Polycarpi* of Heinrich Biber. Edward Tarr and his talented baroque trumpet class led the playing, along with other participants from the workshop. They were accompanied by portative organ and viola da gamba continuo. This was a bold move as not many players were giving public performances on true natural trumpets in those days. Thus arose the tradition of playing as a group at the end of the workshop.

The second turning point—again in Nürnberg—was the inauguration of donations of trumpets to hosting institutions. While working with the participants and demonstrating techniques it is quite feasible for the instructors to assemble an extra

in Bloomington, angeboten. Dort hatten wir eine größere Werkstatt. In dieser Zeit fragte Friedemann Immer nach einem Workshop im Sweelincks Conservatorium in Amsterdam für 1996. Noch heute denken wir zurück, woher wir die Nerven hatten, alle notwendigen Dinge für eine Reise nach Europa zu organisieren, wie z.B. die Verpackung der Werkzeuge in die bereits bekannte große Holzkiste, damit diese im gleichen KLM-Flug mit Robert reist. Aber es hat alles geklappt, obwohl es sehr improvisiert war. Wir danken Friedemann für die Einladung und seine Organisation in Amsterdam. Besonders durch seine Verbindungen in die europäische Trompeterwelt ist alles gut gegangen. Ohne Friedemann hätte sich der nun Internationale Trompeten-bauworkshop in Europa nicht etablieren können.

Im Jahr 1997 gab es drei wichtige Neuerungen. Wir veranstalteten wieder zwei Workshops in Europa. Einer fand in Nürnberg statt, organisiert von Edward Tarr und unterstützt vom Germanischen Nationalmuseum, ein weiterer erneut in Amsterdam. Die erste Neuerung bestand in der musikalischen Präsentation der gebauten Instrumente am Ende des Workshops. Auf dem Programm des öffentlichen Konzertes in der Galerie des Musikinstrumentenmuseums standen u.a. Werke von Girolamo Fantini „Intrada Imperiale" und von Heinrich Biber „Sonata Sancti Polycarpi". Edward Tarr und seine talentierte Barocktrompetenklasse spielten gemeinsam mit den Teilnehmern des Workshops. Das Ensemble wurde von einem Portativ und einer Viola da Gamba als Continuo begleitet. Da es zu dieser Zeit noch nicht viele öffentliche Auftritte mit Naturtrompeten gab, handelte es sich um einen mutigen Schritt. So entstand die Tradition des gemeinsamen musizierens am Ende des Workshops.

trumpet. Such instruments are donated to the hosts, usually with an engraved dedication. The Germanisches National-museum was the first institution to receive one of these gifts, and it was with great pleasure that Bob engraved MACHT IN NVRNBERG on the bell garland.

The third turning point was at the Amsterdam workshop in the Sweelincks Conservatorium where Rick and Bob had the pleasure of meeting and work-ing with Michael Münkwitz, our future collaborator, colleague and friend. Michael impressed us by completing his instrument by mid-Wednesday of the one-week course, complete with beautifully engraved garland and decorated ferrules, and then acting as our assistant for the remainder of the course. This was the start of a dramatic transformation of the workshop.

In 1997 Dr Trevor Herbert, a professor at the Open University in the UK, enrolled in the workshop and brought with him Tony Coe, a producer with the BBC. During the week, while Trevor and the other participants made their instruments, Tony filmed and conducted interviews. The completed half-hour OU/BBC documentary *Getting it Right* was aired several times on BBC 2.

Rick and Bob continued to offer the workshop in Bloomington every year, adding two workshops in Edinburgh in 2002 hosted by Arnold Myers of the Edinburgh University Collection of Historic Musical Instruments. By this time Friedemann Immer had approached us with the proposal that Michael Münkwitz host a workshop in his home town of Rostock, Germany. Bob met Michael and Friedemann at the Historic Brass Society conference in Basel and they shook hands on an agreement that would transform the project. Michael joined Rick and Bob in Edinburgh to act as course assistant and to get a feel for our modus operandi. By

Die zweite Neuerung, die wiederum in Nürnberg ihren Anfang nahm, war die Spende in Form einer Trompete an eine unterstützende Institution. Während des Workshops und der Demonstration der Arbeitsschritte bauten wir gemein-sam als Lehrer eine eigene Trompete, die dann als Spende an die Gastgeber überreicht wurde. Natürlich erhielt die Trompete dann auf dem Kranz eine persönliche Widmung eingraviert. Für Bob war es eine große Freude, die erste Trompete als Geschenk in Nürnberg zu gravieren: „MACHT IN NVRNBERG".

Die dritte Neuerung wurde eingeführt beim Amsterdamer Workshop im Sweelinck Conservatorium, bei dem Bob und Rick Michael Münkwitz, unseren zukünftigen Mitstreiter, Kollegen und Freund trafen. Michael hat uns durch die Fertigstellung seiner Trompete bis Mittwoch Mittag, komplett mit graviert-em Kranz und verzierten Hülsen, über-rascht und uns als Assistent für den Rest des Workshops unterstützt. Der Beginn einer wesentlichen Veränderung für die Zukunft.

1997 waren Dr.Trevor Herbert, Prof. an der Open University in Großbritannien, und mit ihm Tony Coe, Produzent bei der BBC, als Teilnehmer beim Work-shop. Trevor und die Teilnehmer wurden während der Woche gefilmt und gaben Interviews. Die 30-Minuten Dokumentation „Getting in Right" wurde mehrmals bei BBC 2 ausgestrahlt.

Wir fuhren fort, den Workshop jährlich in Bloomington anzubieten. Zusätzlich organisierte Arnold Myers, Edinburgh University, Collection of Historic Musical Instruments , 2002 zwei weitere Workshops in Edinburgh. Zu diesem Zeitpunkt hatte Friedemann Immer vorgeschlagen, in der Heimat-stadt von Michael, Rostock in Mecklenburg-Vorpommern, einen Workshop zu organisieren. Bob und Michael trafen sich bei der Historic

the close of that workshop it was quite clear that Michael would become Our Man in Europe, thus freeing the two originators of the huge logistical problem of shipping heavy crates by air. In effect, this would mean duplicating all the tools and equipment, thus maintaining a complete set on both sides of the Atlantic. And, there would, of course, be an additional teacher, who would take a great load off the two founders.

A most welcome bonus of the Edinburgh workshops was the production of a 'textbook' derived from over 50 photographs taken by Raymond Parks and Jenny Nex. Arnold Myers had sent all participants a contact sheet of prints and it became clear that the processes of the workshop were so well illustrated that a small book would be very straightforward to produce. Arnold kindly offered the services of the Edinburgh University Collection of Historic Musical Instruments as publisher, and in a very short time the book was ready to be included in the workshop registration package. This present book is a more in-depth description of the workshop.

The first test of the European base was a workshop in Kremsmünster in Austria in 2003, which was hosted by Franz Streitweiser, curator of the brass instrument collection at Schloss Kremsegg, followed by a workshop in Rostock the week after. The whole process of driving the entire workshop equipment and materials between European cities had been gone through during the Nürnberg/Amsterdam experience in 1997, so we knew it would be feasible. Michael organized all the equipment, visited the hosting location and set up all the necessary structure for an extremely successful workshop. Workshops in Rostock became a yearly event, using the excellent facilities at the Bildungscentrum der Handwerks-

Brass Society Konferenz in Basel mit Friedemann Immer. Per Handschlag wurde die gemeinsame Zukunft des Internationalen Workshops vereinbart. Michael kam als Assistent nach Edinburgh um ein Gefühl für die gemeinsame Arbeit zu bekommen. Am Ende des Workshops war klar, Michael ist unser Mann in Europa und wir haben damit auch keine Probleme mehr mit dem Versand der schweren Kisten von Übersee.

Ein weiteres Ergebnis war eine zweite komplette Ausrüstung mit allen Werkzeugen und Geräten für beide Seiten des Atlantiks und außerdem durch die Erweiterung des Lehrerteams eine Entlastung der beiden Gründer. Ein sehr willkommener Bonus der Workshops in Edinburgh war die Produktion einer Dokumentation mit über 50 Fotos von Raymond Parks und Jenny Nex. Arnold Myers hat allen Teilnehmern einen Kontaktabzug überreicht und es wurde deutlich, dass die Prozesse des Workshops so gut dargestellt waren, um ein kleines Buch zu produzieren. Arnold bot die Edingburgh University, Collection of Historic Musical Instruments, als Herausgeber an und in sehr kurzer Zeit gehörte das Buch zum Paket für die Teilnehmer des Workshops. Das jetzt vorliegende Buch ist eine Aktualisierung für den bisher sehr erfolgreichen Druck.

Der erste Test des neuen Lehrertrios in Europa waren der Workshop 2003 in Kremsmünster (A), der besonders durch die Unterstützung von Franz Streitwieser (Kurator der Blechblasinstrumentensammlung auf Schloss Kremsegg) zustande kam und ein weiterer danach in Rostock. Durch die beiden Workshops 1997 in Nürnberg und Amsterdam hatten wir Erfahrung im Transport in Europa und waren sicher, beide Wochen hintereinander anbieten zu können. Michael organisierte das zweite Set an Werkzeugen

kammer Mecklenburg-Ostvorpommern. This was an excellent facility with 15 workspaces, and wonderful supporting staff, especially that of Torsten Müller. A further advantage was that accommodation and meals were offered on site, which led to a closer camaraderie between participants.

A second workshop in Kremsmünster followed in 2006. The highlight of that workshop was the moon- and candlelit banquet in the courtyard of the Schloss on the Friday evening, accompanied by 12 trumpets made during the week, and playing music that had been composed for that very place in 1660. It doesn't get any better than that! It was at some time around this period that the title International Trumpet-making Workshop (ITW) became applied. In classic style, Bob really did sketch the logo on the back of an envelope!

Year by year the equipment and tools became more refined. The single bell mandrel was copied several times, so that the workshops in the US and Europe eventually had a set of three each. The system for bending the two bows with Cerrobend (a low-temperature alloy) was upgraded by building thermostatically controlled melting tanks. These also enhanced the safety of the process. Jigs and forms for many of the processes were improved or adapted, and drawing the tubes mechanically improved both quality and efficiency. This streamlining, together with a developing familiarity with the processes and the pacing of the week, meant that construction time was shortened while the quality of the instruments improved. Added decoration was becoming more common as participants found the extra time. By the 15th year of the workshop it was not unusual to see nicely finished and decorated trumpets appearing on the Thursday afternoon of the workshop, thus freeing yet more time for the

und Materialien und besuchte vorab Kremsmünster, um die Arbeitsbedingungen zu besichtigen und alles für einen erfolgreichen Workshop perfekt vorzubereiten. In Rostock hatten wir optimale Bedingungen im Bildungszentrum der Handwerkskammer Mecklenburg-Ostvorpommern. Eine optimal eingerichtete Werkstatt mit 15 Arbeitsplätzen und eine tolle Unterstützung aller Mitarbeiter, besonders des Werkstattleiters Torsten Müller. Ein weiterer Vorteil waren die Übernachtungsmöglichkeiten und Verpflegung im Haus. Viele interessante und freundschaftliche Kontakte entstanden nach der Arbeit beim gemeinsamen Essen und den anschließenden geselligen Runden. Workshops in Rostock wurden ein jährliches Event.

Ein weiterer Workshop in Kremsmünster fand 2006 statt. Der Höhepunkt dieser Woche war das Mond-und Kerzenscheinbankett im Hof des Schlosses, musikalisch begleitet von 12 Trompeten der Teilnehmer. Es wurden Stücke geblasen, die für diesen Ort 1660 komponiert wurden. Es gibt nichts Besseres ! Irgendwann um diese Zeit wurde offiziell der Titel „Internationaler Trompetenbau Workshop" – „ITW" eingeführt. Robert hat tatsächlich, im klassischen Stil, auf der Rückseite eines Briefumschlags das Logo entworfen.

Von Jahr zu Jahr verbesserten sich die Geräte und Werkzeuge. Das einzige Schallstückeisen wurde mehrfach kopiert. So hatten wir in jedem Set 3 Stück zur Verfügung. Das Biegen der beiden Bögen mit Cerobend (Niedertemperatur-Legierung) wurde durch die Anfertigung von elektrischen Thermobehältern vereinfacht. Formen und Kleinwerkzeuge für verschiedene Prozesse wurden ebenfalls verbessert oder angepasst was zu einer erhöhten Instrumentenqualität führte. Eine

making of tuning accessories such as short tuning bits, half-step branches and C-crooks.

The workshops in Bloomington were conducted at the Hoosier Hills Career Center until 2007 when the facility was closed for an extensive renovation. It was decided for the interim to host the ITW in Rick's private workshop, deep in the Indiana State Forest. What was intended as a stop-gap proved so pleasant and convenient that the venue became permanent, so all the North American tools and materials would remain in one place. A bonus was our ability to offer a midday meal on site, thus lessening downtime and creating the convivial atmosphere we had enjoyed in Rostock.

As an add-on to the yearly workshops in Rostock, three workshops hosted by trumpet teacher Juhani Listo were conducted at the South West Finland Art and Craft College in Mynämäki, Finland, between 2005 and 2009. This provided another opportunity to organize all the equipment and materials for the workshop in such a way that they could be transported easily and quickly set up. An overnight ferry trip from Warnemünde to Hanko provided a relaxing interlude between workshops, and also gave Rick the opportunity to compose the *Hainlein Suite (Darstellung des Trompetenbaus)* which had its premiere in Mynämäki, capably played by Juhani and his students. Playing the *Hainlein Suite* at midday on Friday is now a tradition of every workshop.

The Rostock workshops received an extra historical dimension with the discovery by Michael of a trumpet made in 1650 by Wolfram Birckholtz of Nürnberg, a pupil of Hanns Hainlein. He found the instrument hanging in the church in Belitz, a nearby town, as part of a dedication plaque to Jacob Hintze, a trumpeter and inn-keeper who had been

Ziehbank nach alten Vorbildern wurde angefertigt. Diese Erleichterungen und die intensive Auseinandersetzung mit den historischen Techniken führten zu einer Verkürzung der Bauzeit und gleichzeitig zu einem wesentlich besseren Endergebnis. Nach dem 15.Jahr des Workshops war es nicht ungewöhnlich, bereits am Donnerstag Nachmittag die ersten Klänge einer fertigen und gut aussehenden Trompete zu hören.

Bis 2007 wurden die Workshops im Hoosier Hills Career Center angeboten. Danach stand das Zentrum wegen Renovierungen für uns nicht mehr zur Verfügung. Wir suchten nach einer Zwischenlösung und Richard als Gastgeber lud uns in seine eigene Werkstatt in den Wald von Indiana ein. Was als Notlösung gedacht war, bewährte sich und so wurde die private Werkstatt als permanenter Ort für die Workshops in Nord-Amerika. Das Werkzeugset blieb am Ort und ein weiterer Bonus ergab sich. In Richards Werkstatt bekommen alle Teilnehmer Mittagessen, das verringert die Pausen-zeiten und schafft eine ebenso freund-schaftliche Atmosphäre wie in Rostock.

Zusätzlich zum jährlichen Rostocker Workshop konnten wir dreimal zwischen 2005 und 2009 einen Workshop in Süd-West Finnland in der Kunst- und Werkschule in Mynämäki durchführen. Die maßgebliche Organisation lag in den Händen des Trompetenlehrers Juhani Listo. Die anderthalbtägige Überfahrt auf der Fähre von Rostock nach Helsinki zwischen den beiden Wochen war ein willkommenes Zwischenspiel für uns und eine kleine Erholung. Für Richard ergab sich dabei die Gelegenheit eine „Hainlein-Suite" (musikalische Darstellung des Trompetenbauwork-shops) zu komponieren. Ihre Uraufführung erlebte die Suite in Mynämäki, kompetent dargeboten von

killed in a duel. An outcome of this incredible discovery was a project by Rick and Michael to make a set of copies of the instrument, with the research assistance of Markus Raquet in Bamberg, and to stage concerts in the Belitz church. Friedemann Immer and Jean-François Madeuf, who were both participants in the course, presented the first concert in July 2007.

In the following year Jean-François organized a commercial recording in the church featuring four other trumpets, trombone, violone, dulcian, timpani and the church organ. The recording was issued under the Raumklang label. (*Die Birckholtz-trompete von 1650*, Raumklang RK 1805.)

Three further concerts took place between 2008 and 2010. Thus participants in the ITW during those years could experience at first hand the music of instruments of the 17th century before attending the workshop and finding out how the trumpet-making was done. The original Birckholtz trumpet is now displayed in the Musikinstrumenten Sammlung of the Germanisches Nationalmuseum in Nürnberg alongside one of the replicas.

We were approached by Daniel Bangham, director of the Cambridge Woodwind Makers, to put on a workshop in Stapleford, just outside Cambridge, UK in 2012. This involved a shorter ferry trip from Hoek van Holland to Harwich, but a long drive from Rostock in eastern Germany through the Netherlands. The workshop in 2012 had a low attendance, which the three teachers delighted in, as the participants could receive much closer and more individual attention, and it was an opportunity to develop the workshop in a new environment. In the following year, 2013, the participant numbers in Stapleford had increased as word got around.

Juhani Listo und seinen Studenten, die als Teilnehmer eine Trompete gebaut hatten. Traditionell erklingt zum Abschluss der Workshops nun am Freitag Mittag die „Hainlein-Suite".

Die Rostocker Workshops erhielten ab 2007 einen zusätzlichen Programmpunkt durch die Entdeckung der Birckholtz-Trompete (Nürnberg, 1650) durch Michael. Wolfram Birckholtz war Lehrling von Hanns Hainlein. Die Trompete hing viele Jahre unentdeckt in der Dorfkirche von Belitz, südlich von Rostock, an einem Epitaph. Auf dem Gemälde war der Besitzer des Instrumentes, Jacob Hintze, Trompeter und Gastwirt, abgebildet. Dieser wurde in einem Streit getötet. Im Ergebnis dieser fast unglaublichen Entdeckung entwickelte Rick und Michael, mit Unterstützung von Markus Raquet aus Bamberg, die Grundlagen für den Bau von Kopien dieser Trompete. Ein Konzert in der Dorfkirche von Belitz mit den nachgebauten Birckholtz-Trompeten wurde von Jean-Francois Madeuf und Friedemann Immer und Ensemble im Jahr 2007 ein großer Erfolg. Beide waren Teilnehmer des Workshops.

Im folgenden Jahr erweiterte JF Madeuf das Ensemble mit Posaunen, Dulzian, Violinen, Pauken und Orgel. Nach dem Konzert konnten wir in der Kirche eine kommerzielle CD mit dem Label Raumklang produzieren (Die Birckholtz-Trompete von 1650, Raumklang RK 1805). Drei weitere Konzerte fanden zwischen 2008 - 2010 mit unterschiedlichen Besetzungen statt. Die Teilnehmer des ITW konnten so vor Beginn des Workshops in Rostock aus erster Hand die Musik des 17. Jahrhunderts authentisch erleben. Die originale Trompete sowie eine Kopie sind jetzt in der Ausstellung des Musikinstrumentenmuseums im Germanischen Nationalmuseum Nürnberg zu besichtigen.

Nearly 600 instruments have now been completed at the International Trumpet-making Workshop, and a further six have been presented as gifts to hosting institutions. The year 2014 will mark the 20th anniversary and the 50th workshop.

Since 1994 the workshop has been hosted by institutions in the following cities: Bloomington, Indiana, USA; Amsterdam, Netherlands; Nürnberg, Germany; Edinburgh, Scotland; Kremsmünster, Austria; Rostock, Germany; Mynämäki, Finland; Stapleford (Cambridge), England; Schwerin, Germany; and Graz, Austria.

Von Daniel Bangham, Cambridge Woodwind Makers, wurden wir für 2012 zu einem Workshop nach Stapleford, Cambridge (UK) eingeladen. Wieder erwartete uns eine lange Autofahrt von Rostock durch die Niederlande nach Hoek van Holland. Dort setzten wir mit der Fähre nach Harwich über, eine vergleichsweise kurze Schiffsreise. Dieser erste Workshop hatte eine geringe Teilnehmerzahl. Zu unserer Freude konnten wir uns so viel intensiver um die Teilnehmer bemühen und ihnen viel mehr Aufmerksamkeit schenken und unsere Konzepte weiter verfeinern. Der gemeinsame Versuch von Daniel und uns, diesen Trompeten-bau Workshop neben seinen umfang-reichen weiteren Angeboten zu etablieren, hatte Erfolg. Die folgenden Jahre waren gleich nach Bekanntgabe des Termins ausgebucht; das gute Angebot und die Qualität des Work-shops hatten sich herumgesprochen.

Inzwischen haben Teilnehmer aus der ganzen Welt fast 600 Instrumente bei den Internationalen Trompetenbau Workshops gebaut, weitere 6 Trompeten konnten als Spenden an unterstützende Institutionen übergeben werden. Das Jahr 2014 wird unser 20-jähriges Jubiläum und unseren 50. Internationalen Trompetenbau Workshop erleben.

Seit 1994 wurde der Trompetenbau Workshop in folgenden Städten angeboten: Bloomington (USA), Amsterdam (NL), Nürnberg (D), Edinburgh (Schottland), Kremsmünster (A), Rostock (D), Mynämäki (FIN), Stapleford-Cambridge (UK), Schwerin (D), Graz (A).

Section 4
Abschnitt 4

Notes on Materials
Hinweise zu Materialien

Brass
Messing

Copper/Zinc (Cu/Zn) 72/28%, brass sheet 0.4mm thickness
Cupfer/Zink (Cu/Zn) 72/28%, Zuschnitt aus 0,4 mm Messingblech

Silver Solder
Silberlot

Silver (Ag) 40%, remainder brass, melting temp. around 700°C
Silber (AG) 40%, Rest Messing, Schmelztemp. ca. 700° Grad

Silver Solder Flux
Flussmittel zum Hartlöten

Borax (Sodium Borate) $Na_2[B_4O_5(OH)_4]\cdot 8H_2O$
Borax (Natriumborat) $Na_2[B_4O_5(OH)_4]\cdot 8H_2O$

Soft Solder
Zinnlot

Lead/Tin (Pb/Sn) 40/60%, melting temperature around 180°C
Blei/Zinn (Pb/Sn) 40/60%, Schmelzpunkt bei ca. 180° Grad

Soft Solder Flux
Zinnlot Flussmittel

Zinc Chloride solution (ZnCl)
Zinkchloridlösung (ZnCl)

Cerrobend (158 Alloy)
Cerrobend (158 Legierung)

Bismuth (Bi) 50.00%, Lead (Pb) 26.70%, Tin (Sn) 13.30%,
Cadmium (Cd) 10.00%, melting point 70°C
Wismut (Bi) 50.00%, Blei (Pb) 26.70%, Zinn (Sn) 13.30%,
Cadmium (Cd) 10.00%, Schmelzpunkt 70° Grad

Technical drawing
Technische Zeichnung

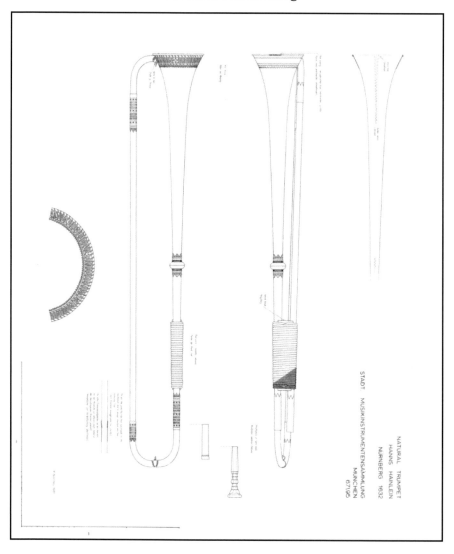

Fig 65. Technical drawing of the Hanns Hainlein trumpet in the Stadtmuseum, Munich
Abb 65. Technische Zeichnung der Hanns Hainlein Trompete im Stadtmuseum, München

Acknowledgements

Danksagung

Firstly we would like to thank the many previous participants who have made instruments with, and anyone reading this who might be interested in future participation. Without their interest and passion for metal-working and music-making none of these workshops would have been possible.

Many of the photographs in this book were taken in 2013 by Michael Münkwitz's son Max during workshops in Rostock and Cambridge, and also at Michael's own workshop in Rostock. A short video describing the workshop was also produced by Max in partnership with Torsten Lenz. The ITW is very grateful to the Stadtmuseum München for the permission to use the technical drawing of the Hanns Hainlein trumpet in its collection.

Trumpeters and teachers Friedemann Immer, Edward Tarr, Juhani Listo and Jean-François Madeuf were all greatly 'instrumental' in the development and success of the ITW through hosting and active participation. Trevor Herbert and Tony Coe produced an excellent and widely aired documentary of the workshop, Franz Streitwieser welcomed us in Austria, and Daniel Bangham offered us his well-equipped workshop in Stapleford. Klaus Martius and Markus Raquet were a great help during the workshop in Nürnberg. We owe thanks to Arnold Myers for document-ation of the workshop during our two weeks in Edinburgh.

We will always be grateful to Prof Randy Long of Indiana University for allowing us the use the silversmith shop in the initial phase of the workshop. Celeste Holler has provided continual unstinting support, especially in the social and organizational aspects of our workshops

Zuerst: Danke an alle bisherigen Teilnehmer und zukünftig Interessierte ! Ohne ihr Interesse und ihre Leiden-schaft für das Handwerk und die Musik wäre der Workshop nicht möglich und eine solche Idee nicht realisierbar! Viele der Fotografien in diesem Buch wurden von Max Münkwitz, Michaels Sohn, während des Workshops in Rostock und Cambridge, sowie in Michaels Werkstatt in Rostock im Jahr 2013 aufgenommen. Den kleinen Film über den Workshop bei youtube produzierten Max und Torsten Lenz. Der ITW ist für die Nutzungserlaubnis der technischen Zeichnung der Hanns Hainlein Trompete sehr dankbar gegenüber dem Stadtmuseum München.

Die Trompeter und Lehrer Friedemann Immer, Edward Tarr, Juhani Listo und Jean-François Madeuf sind alle maßgeblich in die Entwicklung und den Erfolg des ITW eingebunden. Trevor Herbert und Tony Coe produzierten eine hervorragende Dokumentation des Workshops, die bei der BBC ausge-strahlt wurde. Franz Streitwieser hieß uns willkommen in Österreich und Daniel Bangham bot uns seine gut ausgestattete Werkstatt als Dauer-quartier in Großbritannien an. Klaus Martius und Markus Raquet waren eine große Hilfe bei dem Workshop in Nürnberg. Wir schulden Arnold Myers Dank für die Idee der Dokumentation mit Text und Bilder von den beiden Wochen in Edinburgh.

Wir sind immer dankbar Prof. Randy Long von der Indiana University für die unkomplizierte Unterstützung und Nutzungsmöglichkeit der Silber-schmiedewerkstatt bei der Startphase dieser Idee. Celeste Holler, die gute Fee, die uns bei den Workshops in

in Bloomington. Finally, we thank all the friends and partners who have supported us over many years, and we apologize to those who might have been left off this long list.

Bloomington organisatorisch und menschlich die Basis für unsere Arbeit gibt. Wir danken allen ungenannten Freunden und Partnern, die uns über die vielen Jahre unterstützt haben und entschuldigen uns, wenn wir versehentlich eine wichtige Person auf dieser Liste vergessen haben, aber die Breite und Vielzahl eines solchen Projektes schließt Fehler leider nicht aus.

Bibliography
Bibliographie

Altenburg, J.E., *Versuch einer Anleitung zur heroisch-musikalischen Trompeter-und Pauker-Kunst* (Halle, 1795). (Translation by E. H. Tarr, The Brass Press, 1974)

Baines, A., *Brass Instruments* (London: Faber and Faber, 1976)

Barclay, R., The Art of the *Trumpet-maker: The Materials, Tools and Techniques of the 17th and 18th Centuries in Nuremberg*, Early Music Series 14 (Oxford: Oxford University Press, 1992)

Barclay, R., "A New Species of Instrument: The Vented Trumpet in Context", *Historic Brass Society Journal*, 10, 1998, pp. 1-13.

Bate, P., *The Trumpet and Trombone* (London: Ernest Benn, 1978)

Halle, J.S., *Werkstätte der heutigen Künste*, Band III (Brandenburg and Leipzig: J. W. & J. S. Halle, 1764)

Klaus, S. K., *Trumpets and Other High Brass* (Vermillion, SD: National Music Museum, 2012)

Klein, J.G.F., *Beschreibung der Metall-Lothe und Löthungen* (Berlin: 1760)

Seraphinoff, R., "Compromise and Authenticity in the Baroque Trumpet and Horn", *Posaunen und Trompeten*, Michaelsteiner Konferenzberichte, (Blankenburg: Stiftung Kloster Michaelstein, 2001), pp. 199-206.

Weigel, C., *Abbildung der gemein nützlichen Hauptstände* (Regensburg: 1698)

Wörthmüller, W., "Die Nürnberger Trompeten- und Posaunenmacher des 17. und 18. Jahrhunderts", *Mittelungen des Vereins für Geschichte der Stadt Nürnberg*, 45 (1954)

Contacts
Kontakte

www.seraphinoff.com/itw
www.trompetenmacher.de/itw
www.loosecannonpress.com

CPSIA information can be obtained
at www.ICGtesting.com
Printed in the USA
LVIC06n1221090614
389224LV00002B/2